On the Job™

with a

POLICE OFFICER
PROTECTOR OF THE PEACE

Jonathan Rubinstein
Illustrated by Susan Gal

BARRON'S

First edition for the United States and Canada published
exclusively by Barron's Educational Series, Inc. in 2001

All inquiries should be addressed to:
Barron's Educational Series, Inc.
250 Wireless Boulevard
Hauppauge, NY 11788
http://www.barronseduc.com

Library of Congress Catalog Card No. 2001135066

International Standard Book No. 0-7641-1870-6

Printed in Singapore
9 8 7 6 5 4 3 2 1

POLICE OFFICER
PROTECTOR OF THE PEACE

Meet Bridgit and Hugo.

They are friends and neighbors. Together they guide readers through the exciting world of various careers.

• •

In *On the Job with a Police Officer*, Bridgit and Hugo meet Bob Miller and Marie Sanchez, patrol officers who recover a stolen handbag. Bridgit and Hugo visit the officers at police headquarters and learn the nitty-gritty of what it takes to be a police officer.

• •

Table of Contents

On the Scene

Bridgit and Hugo are standing in front of the Sweet Shop, enjoying their ice cream cones. Suddenly, speeding around the corner out of nowhere, a bike rider knocks a woman down, grabs her handbag, and pedals off as fast as he can. The woman lies sprawled on the ground.

"He knocked her down on purpose, Bridgit," Hugo shouts. "Did you see that?" Both kids run over to the woman, who is shaken and crying. Hugo stays with her while Bridgit finds a pay phone and dials 911.

"A woman was knocked down by a bike rider," she says. "He stole her purse. We're at the corner of Beech and Palmer, and he's headed toward Willow... He was wearing a sweatshirt. The bike? I'm not sure of the color...red, maybe... No, I didn't get a good look at him. He was wearing a hood... Yes ma'am, I'll stay right here with her."

A few moments later, a police car arrives. Two officers get out of the car and walk over to where Hugo and Bridgit are standing with the woman. "I'm Officer Bob Miller, and this is my partner, Officer Marie Sanchez," Officer Miller says. "What's your name, ma'am?"

"Ellen McGrath, officer," she says.

"We found your purse, Ms. McGrath," Officer Sanchez says. "Thanks to whoever called 911."

"The robber got scared and left the bag and the bike just around the corner," Officer Miller says, handing Ms. McGrath the purse. "Would you check to see if anything is missing?"

"My wallet, my money, it's all here. Thanks to these wonderful kids," she says, hugging Hugo and Bridgit.

Just call me super-pooch, protector of purses!

Staying in Touch

Everything police officers need to do their jobs is in their car. Police cars are equipped with special computers that let them get information about motor vehicles and their drivers. Police cars also have special radios that let the officers stay in touch with their dispatcher and with the other officers on patrol in the area. When Bridgit called 911, the operator used a police radio to contact Officers Miller and Sanchez, and send them to the scene. When officers aren't in their car, they take portable radios with them wherever they go.

Officer Sanchez takes Bridgit and Hugo to sit in the car, so they can answer a few questions.

"You did great, Bridgit," Officer Sanchez says. "Telling the dispatcher who took your call which way the bike was heading put us right there. The thief got scared when he heard the siren. You're eyewitnesses. Anything you can tell us is important. You might help us identify the robber. Hugo, did you see the rider's face?" she asks.

"No way," Hugo replies. "He was too far away. All I saw was that hooded sweatshirt. It happened so fast. I don't even know the color," he admits.

"Did it look like this one?"
Officer Sanchez asks, holding up
an orange sweatshirt.

"Yeah!" both kids shout. "That's it."

"He ditched it, and you were right, Bridgit, the bike is red!
You kids sure saved the day for Ms. McGrath,"
Officer Sanchez says.

"You kids have already been a great help.
We'd like to give you a special thank you.
Would you like to go for a ride in our
squad car, and come see headquarters?"

"That would be cool," Hugo says, "but we have
to call home and get permission, first."

CHAPTER 2

Going Downtown

While Hugo and Bridgit call home, Officer Miller finishes interviewing Ms. McGrath and joins them in the car. On their way to headquarters, the officers take Bridgit and Hugo on a tour of the area they patrol, which they call their "beat."

"We spend most of our time in this neighborhood. We try hard to get to know the people who live and work here, so that when something unusual happens, we notice it fast," Officer Miller says.

"It feels great to be a part of this community, and to know that the work we do helps the people we know," Officer Sanchez says.

No two days are alike for beat officers.
They take turns protecting the people
on their patrol, day and night. They help out
however they can: directing traffic, helping
settle arguments before they turn into
fights, and dealing with crowds at events
like parades and festivals. They respond
to crimes in progress, and try to
make the streets safer by stopping
crimes before they start.

"Patrol officers work in teams and count on their partners. Marie and I know a lot about each other: how we look at things, our strengths and weaknesses. Like the fact that I have better night vision than she does, and that Marie runs faster than I do," Officer Miller says.

Officers Miller and Sanchez are in the patrol division of the local police department in a big city. But there are patrol officers in small towns and rural areas, too. Forest rangers and game wardens enforce the laws in wilderness areas.

There are sheriffs who are responsible for a whole county, and state troopers who can work anywhere around a state. Police officers also work for the federal government, investigating special crimes like counterfeiting and mail fraud.

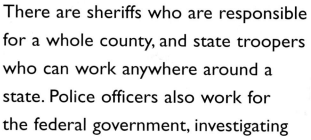

I smell something funny about this money!

The First Force

Until about 150 years ago, crime victims were themselves responsible for investigating and prosecuting criminals. Some people hired professional "thief-catchers" to recover stolen property. The first police force was formed in 1829 in London, England. American cities soon did the same, and now there are police departments all over the world. British police officers are known as bobbies, in honor of their founder, Sir Robert (Bobby) Peel.

CHAPTER 3
Headquarters

The police car pulls up outside a large building.

"This is headquarters, kids. It's the center of all of the police work we do. Officers come here to get their assignments. This is also where we bring the people who have been arrested before they go to court," Officer Sanchez says.

PUBLIC SAFETY BUILDING

The officers take Bridgit and Hugo on a tour of the station. The first stop is the radio room, the nerve center of the police force.

Uh-oh... I'd better be a good dog!

"When there's an emergency, the 911 call comes here." Officer Miller says. "Bridgit talked to a dispatcher working right in this room."

The group moves on to the records room, where they see a row of cabinets filled with criminal records, along with pictures and fingerprints of people who have been arrested.

"Fingerprinting is an important part of police work," says Officer Sanchez. "It's still the best way to identify people."

"Nobody else in the whole world has fingerprints like mine?" Hugo asks.

"That's right," Officer Sanchez answers.

"The person who pushed Ms. McGrath down and took her pocketbook was not arrested, so a copy of the police report comes to this office. The crime analysts pinpoint the incident on a map, along with others that have

happened around the same time. Criminals have habits. We try to find patterns in the crimes we see," Officer Miller says.

"And that tells you where to look for problems in the future?" Hugo asks.

"Exactly. We can't be everywhere all the time, so it helps to know the best areas to look for trouble," Officer Sanchez says.

"Police officers arrest people they suspect of a crime.
They collect evidence. Finally, they testify in court about what they
know or have seen concerning a crime. It is up to a judge and jury to
decide guilt or innocence."

"Even if you had caught someone with Ms. McGrath's purse and the
bike, it wouldn't have proven his guilt?" Hugo asks.

"Maybe not. He could have found the bike and the purse after the
thief ditched it," Sanchez says. "Remember, you couldn't identify
anyone, right?" Hugo and Bridgit nod.

In the crime lab, detectives examine any evidence that's been collected to try to learn the whole story. "If we had arrested a suspect, we would have tried to match fingerprints on the stolen bag with those on the bike. We would also see whether clothing fibers or hair from the victim was present on the suspect's clothes or hands. If so, that would connect the suspect with the crime," Officer Miller says.

"Wow!" exclaims Bridgit. "I thought all you did was chase bad guys and go on stake-outs. How do you learn all the different things you need to know?"

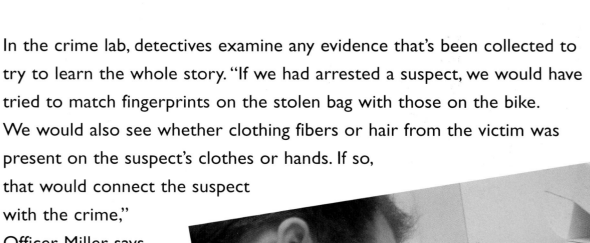

CHAPTER 4

Job Training

"To become a police officer, you have to attend a police academy," Officer Miller says.

Police training lasts six months. Students study the law, crime scene and accident analysis, evidence collection, and problem solving. They learn how to ask the right questions to get the information they need, and to write reports clearly.

At many police academies, students live in dormitories. They train five or six days a week. They clean their rooms and make their beds every morning, then shower and stand for inspection before breakfast. Once or twice a day, they exercise or jog.

"I guess you have to be really strong to be a police officer," Bridgit says.

"You have to be fit," Officer Sanchez says, "but you don't have to be all muscle. You must be healthy and in good physical condition, so you can help someone who has been injured in an accident, or stand up to someone who is resisting arrest."

"Besides, Bridgit, police have guns and sticks, and all kinds of stuff to fight bad guys with," Hugo adds.

"You have the wrong idea, Hugo. We train to use the weapons we carry, but we never use more force than we have to. Never," Officer Miller says firmly. "In fact, most police officers never fire their guns."

Besides learning how and when to use their weapons, students train for other emergency situations. They learn rescue techniques, first aid, and how to drive safely at high speeds. Students also learn how to work as a team and how to trust their partners.

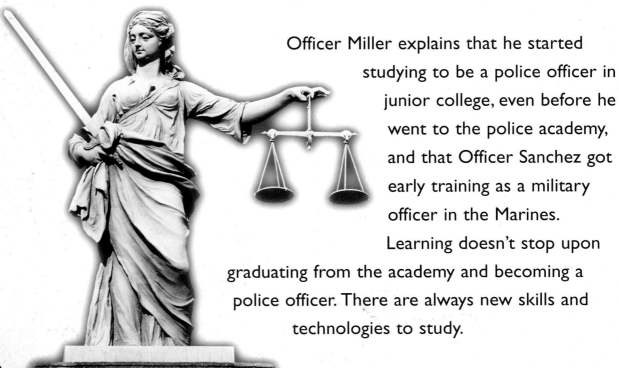

Officer Miller explains that he started studying to be a police officer in junior college, even before he went to the police academy, and that Officer Sanchez got early training as a military officer in the Marines.

Learning doesn't stop upon graduating from the academy and becoming a police officer. There are always new skills and technologies to study.

"Many of my friends on the force are taking classes in their spare time," Officer Sanchez says. "Psychology, photography, computers, accounting, science, communications…"

"You mean they're learning everything they can to help people and to prevent crime," Bridgit interjects.

"I'd say Bridgit is thinking like a police officer," Officer Sanchez says, smiling.

Saying Good-Bye

"If I wanted to be a police officer, what's the most important thing I could do right now?" Hugo asks.

"Study hard, don't lie or break the law, and practice being kind and helpful," Officer Miller says.

"Police work is not for everyone," Officer Sanchez says. "Without honesty, modesty, and a love of hard work, plus an interest in a bit of adventure, you'd better look for a different job."

"Marie and I know you both have what it takes. You showed that when you helped Ms. McGrath," Officer Miller says.

To thank Bridgit and Hugo for their help, Officers Miller and Sanchez give the kids Official Junior Police Officer badges.

"It wouldn't surprise me if in a dozen years, after you've graduated from college, I'll be saying, 'Hey, Rookie, how do you like this job?'" Officer Sanchez adds, grinning at Bridgit and Hugo.

Activities

Being a police officer is a challenging job that requires having a special set of abilities and being a special kind of person. You might be surprised at how many of the most important skills and qualities you already have.

- Do you notice little details about the things that are happening around you?

- Can you tell a story so that it is easy to understand?

- Do you like to solve mysteries?

Try the following activities on your own, with a partner, or with a group of friends, and find out if you have what it takes to be a police officer!

ACTIVITY 1

Scene of the Crime

Look at the drawing on the next page for about a minute, or until you think you can recall the details. Then write a description of what you remember. The questions below may jog your memory.

- What are the streets at the intersection called?

- What time does the clock say?

- How many people and dogs are on the street?

- What other things do you remember being in the street?

- How many people can you see at the windows and doors of the buildings?

- What does the sky look like?

Make a Report

Police officers need to report facts clearly and accurately. They are taught to answer six questions in their reports: who, what, when, where, why, and how. "Why" is often the hardest question to answer. The reason someone commits a crime is called the *motive*.

Write a report of what happened to Ellen McGrath. Just as a police officer would, put in your report what Bridgit and Hugo saw the bike rider do.

You should be able to describe what, when, where, and how the incident happened, but you won't know who and why. Without knowing who pushed Ms. McGrath and took her purse, you can't discover the motive for doing it.

ACTIVITY 3
Memory Sketch

There is a big difference between just seeing your surroundings and carefully observing them.

Sketch a classroom from memory, filling in as many details as you can.

- How many rows of desks are there?

- Where is the clock? What else is on the walls?

- How many windows are there?

- What other details can you add?

Take your sketch to class and compare it to the real thing.

- What did you leave out?

- What did you remember incorrectly?

Repeating this activity for other places will help you notice and remember your surroundings more.

ACTIVITY 4 Stakeout

Pick a partner and find a place where you can both sit comfortably without being noticed. You're on a stakeout, observing what the people passing by look like and what they are doing.

After a while, take turns being witnesses, just like in court, by asking each other questions about what you have observed.

- How many people walked by?

- How many were walking their dogs?

- What did the man walking the terrier look like?

- Was the dog's tail wagging?

What did you notice that your friend didn't, and vice versa? After you have compared notes, it's time to put your spy sunglasses back on and get back to your stakeout.

ACTIVITY 5

Ear-witness

The more kids who participate in this activity, the better.

Write down a simple story that's two or three sentences long. Here's one: "The big, blue car was parked on top of the hill, when suddenly its brakes gave out. It rolled down the hill and knocked over a silver garbage can and a red mailbox, and it smashed a crate of jelly donuts." Put in enough details to make all of them tough to remember.

The big, blue car was parked

Ask everyone to sit in a circle. Whisper the story to the kid on your left. This kid whispers the story to the next kid, and so on, until everyone has heard it. The last kid to hear the story says it aloud for the whole group to hear. Then it's time to reread the original story and see how much the story has changed in the telling.

top of the hill, when ...

ACTIVITY 6 — Obstacle Course

Build an obstacle course in your backyard or a nearby park, so you can practice the kinds of tricky moves that patrol officers know how to make. Scramble over a picnic table, crawl under a bench, hop over a row of Frisbees, jump over a stack of stones.

Or instead of creating your own course, try picking a route through a playground that takes you over, under, around, and through tunnels, ladders, and other obstacles.

The idea is to test your agility and physical fitness.

I can do that with my eyes closed!

ACTIVITY 7

Partners

Police officers often patrol their beats in teams. Pick a partner and see how well you can work together.

Take a bandanna or short piece of rope and tie your left ankle to your partner's right ankle. Make the knot tight enough to keep your feet together, but not so tight that it cuts off circulation.

Practice walking and jogging with your ankles tied together. To test your cooperation skills even further, try moving (slowly and carefully) through the obstacle course you built in Activity 6.

Anti-Crime Cleanup

Does your neighborhood have litter on its streets or graffiti on its walls? They're both against the law—and they're messy and ugly!

Organize a group of friends to pick up litter once a week. Cleaner streets mean fewer people will throw their trash there.

Find out from local police headquarters whether there's an anti-graffiti program you can join. If not, form your own. Ask around for donations of paint and brushes, gloves and masks, and safe cleaning solutions. Get permission from wall owners, then gather a team and get to work. Less graffiti means less graffiti drawn.

What a mess Hugo and Bridgit have gotten me into!

The job of police officers is to make their communities safer, better places to live and work.

What can you do to make your neighborhood safer and better?

- Do broken streetlights need fixing?

- Are there dangerous cracks and bumps in the sidewalk?

Ask an adult or the police officer on your beat to find out who to call to get the lights and sidewalks repaired, then make the call.

Glossary

Cadet
What a police officer in training is sometimes called.

Dispatcher
The person who answers emergency telephone calls from residents, and then sends police officers to the scene to help solve the problem.

Evidence
Information or material that proves whether a statement or idea is true or false. If your mother finds cookie crumbs on the couch, it is evidence that someone was eating in the living room.

Eyewitness
A person who sees an event take place. His or her version of the event counts in a court of law as evidence about what happened.

Fingerprint
No two people have the same fingerprints—the pattern of lines, loops, and swirls on the tips of their fingers. The police can trace fingerprints to people who touched objects at a particular location.

Headquarters
The central base of operations for a police department, where radio dispatchers, crime lab technicians, patrol officers, and other members of the police force work together.

Investigation
The process of collecting evidence and interviewing witnesses to try to find out the facts of a case.

Suspect
A person whom the police believe may have committed a crime, based on the evidence collected.

Testify
To tell one's version of the facts of a case in front of a judge and/or jury.

Resources

Careers in Policing

For information about careers in law enforcement near you, contact your local, county, and state law enforcement agencies or the nearest branch of the Federal Bureau of Investigation (FBI).

Being a Police Officer

Colleen Stanley Bare
Sammy, Dog Detective
New York: Cobblehill, 1998

Donna M. Jackson
The Bone Detectives: How Forensic Anthropologists Solve Crimes and Uncover Mysteries of the Dead
New York: Little, Brown, 2001

Lois Lenski
Policeman Small
New York: Random House, 2001

Christine Osinski and Alice K. Flannagan
Officer Brown Keeps Neighborhoods Safe
New York: Children's Press, 1998

Dee Ready and Dolores Ready
Police Officers: Community Helpers
Mankato, Minn.: Bridgestone Books, 1997

The books in this series are produced by Orange Avenue, Inc.
Creative Director: Hallie Warshaw
Writer: Jonathan Rubinstein
Contributing Writer: Jake Miller
Design & Production: Britt Menendez, B Designs
Illustrator: Susan Gal
Editor: Robyn Brode
Photographer: Emily Vassos
Creative Assistant: Emily Vassos
Models: Mike Baraz, Peggy Butz, Jacqueline Graf, and Tanya Napier

Consultants: Dave Epstein, former police chief, Savannah, Georgia, and Travis Miller, a public safety consultant, Waltham, Massachusetts

Special Thanks to: Angel Bernal and the Mill Valley Police Department

Photo Credits: Corbis, Eyewire, Gettyone.com, Photodisc, and Picture Quest